Beginner Biography

Maria Tallchief

Native America's Prima Ballerina

by Jennifer Marino Walters

illustrated by Nigel Dobbyn and Daniela Geremia

LOOK!
BOOKS™

Red Chair Press   Egremont, Massachusetts

Look! Books are produced and published by Red Chair Press:

Red Chair Press LLC   PO Box 333   South Egremont, MA 01258-0333

www.redchairpress.com

 FREE lesson guide at www.redchairpress.com/free-activities

Publisher's Cataloging-In-Publication Data
Names: Marino Walters, Jennifer, author. | Dobbyn, Nigel, illustrator.
Title: Maria Tallchief : Native America's prima ballerina / by Jennifer
Marino Walters ; illustrated by Nigel Dobbyn.

Description: Egremont, Massachusetts : Red Chair Press, [2020] | Series:
   Look! books. Beginner biography | Includes index, glossary, and
   resources for further reading. | Interest age level: 006-009. |
   Summary: "Maria Tallchief knew she wanted to dance while watching Osage
   dancers as a child in Oklahoma. For tribal ceremonies, only men were
   allowed to dance. But, Maria went on to become America's first prima
   ballerina. She was one of the best dancers in the world"--Provided by
   publisher.

Identifiers: ISBN 9781634409995 (library hardcover) | ISBN 9781634400497
   (paperback) | ISBN 9781634407250 (ebook)

Subjects: LCSH: Tallchief, Maria--Juvenile literature. | Indian
ballerinas--United States--Biography--Juvenile literature. | Osage
Indians--United States--Biography--Juvenile literature. | CYAC:
Tallchief, Maria. | Ballerinas--United States--Biography. | Osage
Indians--United States--Biography.

Classification: LCC GV1785.T32 M37 2020 (print) | LCC GV1785.T32 (ebook) |
   DDC 792.8/028/092 B--dc23

Library of Congress Control Number : 2019940526

Photo credits: p. 4: Jacob Harris/AP Images; p. 14: John Rooney/ AP Images

Printed in the United States of America

0420 1P CGF20

Table of Contents

A Native American Childhood

Elizabeth Marie (Maria) Tall Chief was born on January 24, 1925 in Fairfax, Oklahoma. Her father was a member of the Osage Indian tribe. Her mother had a Scottish-Irish background. The family lived on an **Indian reservation**.

Back then, many Native American customs were against the law. So tribes gathered secretly to watch the men do traditional Indian dances. Osage women did not dance.

Music in Her Heart

But Maria was not like other Native American girls and women. She and her younger sister, Marjorie, started taking piano and ballet lessons when they were very young. They practiced for hours each day.

When Maria was 8, the family moved to Los Angeles, California.

Hard Work

At age 12, Maria decided to focus only on ballet. She began to study under well-known Russian ballerina Bronislava Nijinska. All the great ballet dancers at that time were from Russia.

Madame Nijinska was very strict. She had Maria and the other students work very hard.

9

A Dream is Born

In 1938, the Ballet Russe de Monte Carlo came to Los Angeles. That group included the very best Russian ballet dancers. Maria went to every performance. She decided her dream was to join the Ballet Russe.

After World War II began in Europe, Ballet Russe performed in cities across the United States.

A Dream Comes True

In 1942, Maria's dream came true. After graduating from high school at age 17, she went to New York and joined Ballet Russe.

Unlike many American dancers, Maria refused to adopt a Russian stage name. She was proud of her American Indian heritage. But she did combine her last name into one word, Tallchief.

A Marriage

Maria quickly became known for her incredible **technique**, grace, and speed. When famous **choreographer** George Balanchine became a leader of Ballet Russe, he quickly noticed her talent— and her beauty. Maria and George got married in 1946.

Prima Ballerina

In 1947, Maria left Ballet Russe. She then joined her husband's new Ballet Society, which became the New York City Ballet. Maria became its first **prima ballerina**.

George created many great roles for Maria. These included the Swan Queen in "Swan Lake" and the Sugar Plum Fairy in "The Nutcracker." After Maria and George divorced in 1952, she stayed with the New York City Ballet until she retired from the stage in 1965.

Big Honors

In 1974, Maria founded, or began, a ballet school in Chicago, Illinois. She also served as artistic director of the Chicago City Ballet from 1981 to 1987.

In 1996, Maria was **inducted** into the National Women's Hall of Fame. She received a Kennedy Center Honor that same year.

19

Trailblazer

Maria died in 2013 at age 88. Maria Tallchief will always be remembered as a **trailblazer** for Native Americans. With a lot of hard work, she fought back against discrimination to become America's first prima ballerina— and one of the greatest ballerinas of the 20th century.

Timeline: Big Dates in Maria's Life

1925: Maria is born in Fairfax, Oklahoma.

1933: Maria and her family move to Los Angeles, California.

1942: After graduating from Beverly Hills High School, she joins Ballet Russe de Monte Carlo in New York.

1946: Maria marries famous choreographer George Balanchine. They later divorce.

1947: She leaves Ballet Russe and joins the Ballet Society, which becomes the New York City Ballet.

1956: Maria marries Henry D. Paschen, Jr. Their daughter, Elise, is born three years later.

1965: Maria retires from dancing.

1974: She opens the ballet school of the Lyric Opera in Chicago.

1996: Maria is inducted into the National Women's Hall of Fame and receives a Kennedy Center Honor.

2013: Maria dies in Chicago at age 88.

Words to Know

choreographer: a person who arranges dances

Indian reservation: an area of land that is set aside for Native Americans by the U.S. government

inducted: placed into

prima ballerina: the leading female dancer in a ballet or ballet company

technique: the way in which physical movements or skills are used

trailblazer: someone who prepares the way for others who follow

Learn More at the Library

(Check out these books to read with others.)

Doyle, Alice. *Maria Tallchief, Grade K History Leveled Reader.* Houghton Mifflin, 2005.

Gourley, Catherine. *Who Was Maria Tallchief?* Penguin Workshop, 2002.

Tallchief, Maria; Wells, Rosemary. *Tallchief: America's Prima Ballerina.* Puffin, 2001.

Index

About the Author

Jennifer Marino Walters loves to dance when no one is looking. She and her husband live with their twin boys and daughter in the Washington D.C. area. While Jennifer may hide her dancing from others, her young daughter is happy to show her skills as a ballerina to anyone who asks.